AF270611

Stellar Space
Famous Space Missions
by Julie Murray
3
Dash!
LEVELED READERS
An Imprint of Abdo Zoom • abdobooks.com

Level 1 – Beginning
Short and simple sentences with familiar words or patterns for children who are beginning to understand how letters and sounds go together.

Level 2 – Emerging
Longer words and sentences with more complex language patterns for readers who are practicing common words and letter sounds.

Level 3 – Transitional
More developed language and vocabulary for readers who are becoming more independent.

abdobooks.com

Published by Abdo Zoom, a division of ABDO, PO Box 398166, Minneapolis, Minnesota 55439. Copyright © 2022 by Abdo Consulting Group, Inc. International copyrights reserved in all countries. No part of this book may be reproduced in any form without written permission from the publisher. Dash!™ is a trademark and logo of Abdo Zoom.

Printed in the United States of America, North Mankato, Minnesota.
052021
092021

Photo Credits: Alamy, iStock, NASA, Science Source, Shutterstock
Production Contributors: Kenny Abdo, Jennie Forsberg, Grace Hansen, John Hansen
Design Contributors: Candice Keimig, Neil Klinepier, Victoria Bates

Library of Congress Control Number: 2020919492

Publisher's Cataloging in Publication Data

Names: Murray, Julie, author.
Title: Famous space missions / by Julie Murray
Description: Minneapolis, Minnesota : Abdo Zoom, 2022 | Series: Stellar space | Includes online resources and index.
Identifiers: ISBN 9781098226251 (lib. bdg.) | ISBN 9781098226398 (ebook) | ISBN 9781098226466 (Read-to-Me ebook)
Subjects: LCSH: Outer space--Juvenile literature. | Outer space--Exploration--Juvenile literature. | Missions (Astronautics)--Juvenile literature. | Orbital transfer (Space flight)--Juvenile literature.
Classification: DDC 629.45--dc23

Table of Contents

The Beginning

Missions have launched into space for more than 60 years. The missions have discovered new **galaxies**. They have widened our understanding of the universe. They have even allowed humans to live in space!

Sputnik 1 was the first man-made **satellite** in space. The **Soviet Union** launched it on October 4, 1957. It **orbited** Earth for three weeks before its batteries died.

ИСКУССТВЕННЫЙ СПУТНИК ЗЕМЛИ
THE FIRST EARTH SPUTNIK
2
7

Apollo 11 was the first flight to put humans on the moon. The lunar lander touched down on July 20, 1969. Neil Armstrong and Buzz Aldrin were the first humans to step foot on the moon.

Exploring Space

The Hubble Space Telescope went into **orbit** in 1990. It has discovered new moons and **exoplanets**. It has also helped us understand how **galaxies** and planets form.

The Cassini-Huygens mission launched in 1997. It studied Saturn's rings and many moons. The Huygens probe landed on Saturn's largest moon, Titan. It studied Titan's **atmosphere**, clouds, and surface.

Spirit and Opportunity were a pair of rovers that landed on Mars in January 2004. They found clues that water had once been on the Red Planet.

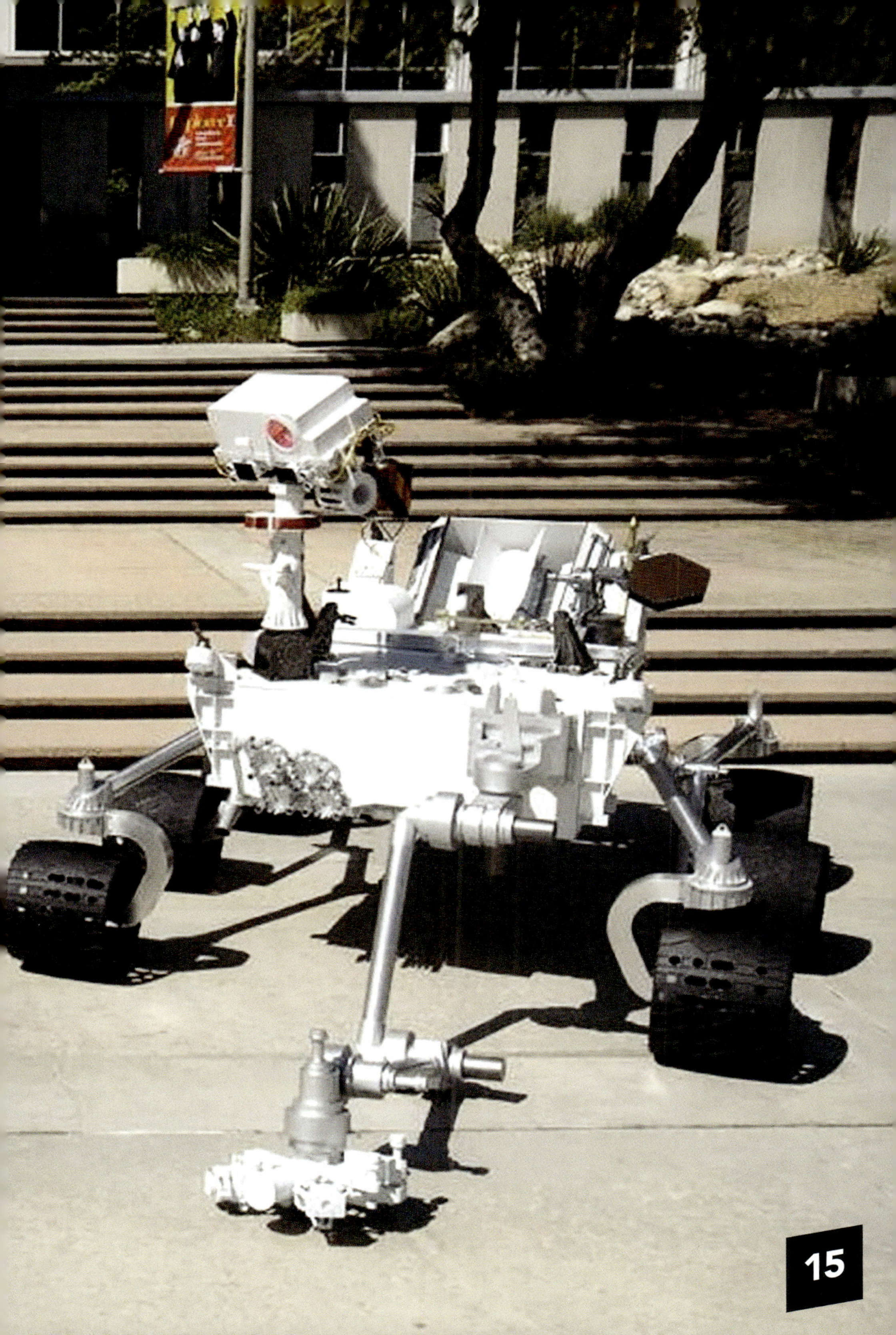

Curiosity rover landed on Mars in August 2012. Curiosity is the size of a car. Its mission is to find out if Mars ever had the right conditions to support small life forms.

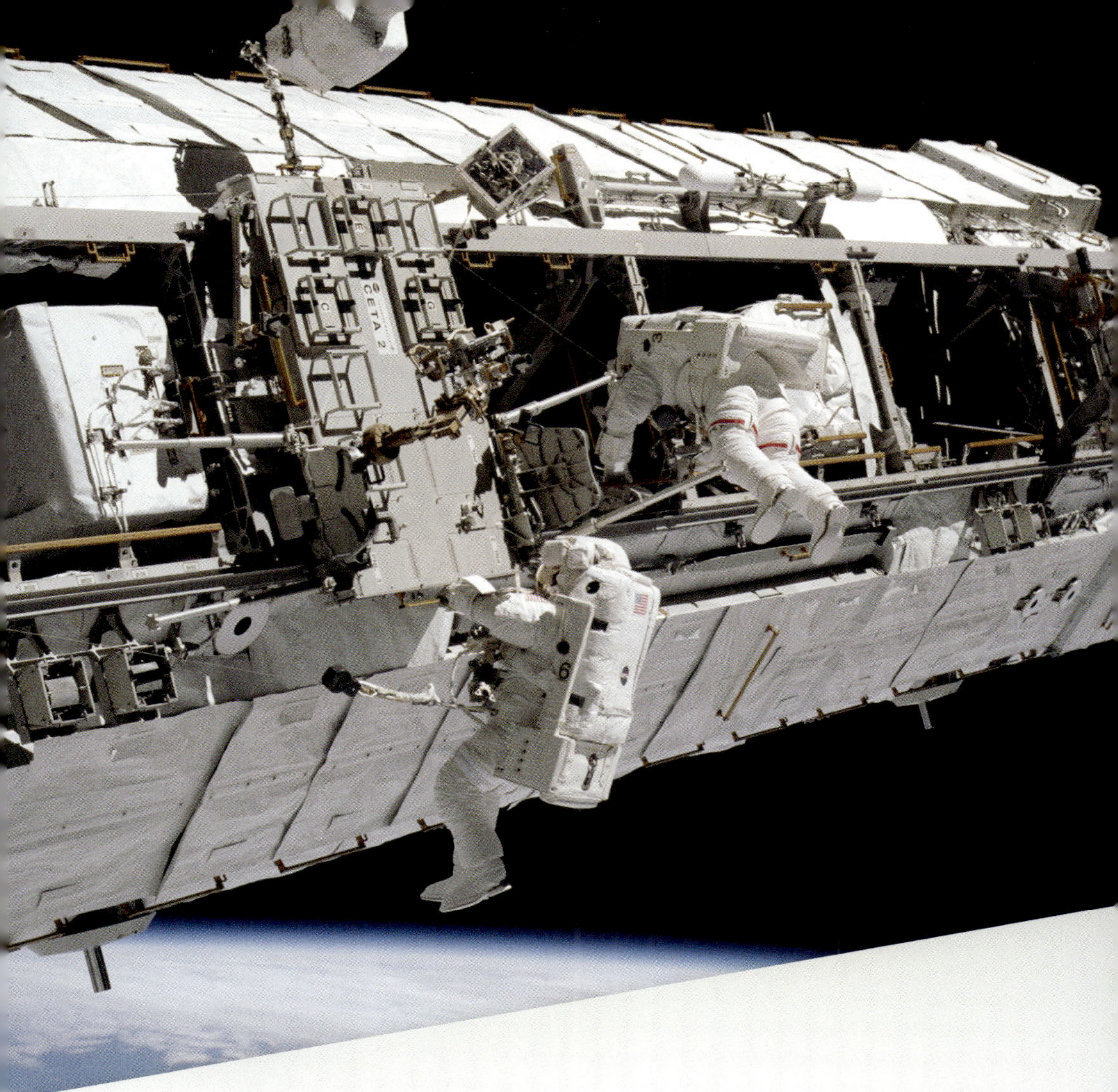

The International Space Station (ISS) is a **satellite** and research laboratory. It currently **orbits** Earth once every 90 minutes! Astronauts from around the world live and work on the ISS.

Disaster

Not all missions have been successful. The Challenger disaster took place on January 28, 1986. The space shuttle broke apart 73 seconds into flight. All seven crew members tragically died on the mission.

More Space Missions

- **Vostok 1 (1961)** – first manned spaceflight in history with Yuri Gagarin aboard

- **Voyager program (launched 1977)** – includes two probes, Voyager 1 and 2, that collect data and send it to Earth

- **Chandra X-Ray Observatory (launched 1999)** – space telescope that has observed black holes, supernovas, and new galaxies

- **Mars 2020 (Launched July 2020)** – Perseverance rover, landed February 2021, collects samples of rock and soil for return to Earth

Glossary

atmosphere – the gases surrounding the earth or similar objects in outer space.

exoplanet – a planet that orbits a star that is not our sun.

galaxy – a collection of billions of stars and other matter held together by gravity. Our planet Earth and the sun belong to the Milky Way galaxy. They are only tiny parts of this galaxy.

orbit – to move in a circle around.

satellite – a spacecraft that is sent into orbit around a planet or other heavenly body.

Soviet Union – a country that no longer exists that was made up of fifteen republics in eastern Europe and northern Asia. Moscow was its capital.

Index

Online Resources

To learn more about the famous space missions, please visit **abdobooklinks.com** or scan this QR code. These links are routinely monitored and updated to provide the most current information available.